Gibbon Island

Story by Beverley Randell   Illustrations by Julian Bruère

Two gibbons and their baby
lived in a cage at the zoo.

Sometimes they swung
from an old branch
with their long arms.
They had nothing else to do,
because they couldn't go outside.

"That cage is much too small
for gibbons," said the young keeper.
"They need **tall** trees to climb.
Gibbons love to climb up high."

"I think we could put the gibbons
on the island in the lake
where the pelicans live,"
said the head keeper.
"Then they wouldn't need
to be inside a cage at all.
Gibbons never try to swim."

"The gibbons would love being outside,"
said the young keeper.
"But we will have to make
the lake deeper.
That would stop people
from walking over
to the island."

Soon a digger came to move dirt
out of the lake.
All the wet dirt
was dropped on the island.

The lake grew deeper,
and the island grew higher.

Some children came to watch.

People planted trees on the island.

"Wild gibbons live in rainforests,"
the keeper told the children.
"We are trying to make the island
look like their home in the wild."

The work went on for many weeks.
Builders came to make a new house
for the gibbons
at the side of the lake.
It would be a warm, safe place
for the gibbons to sleep in at night.

They built a little bridge
from the house to the island.

When it was time to move the gibbons,
the head keeper said,
"We must be very careful.
The gibbons have never lived
outside a cage before.
They could be scared at first.
Then they might rush around too fast
and hurt themselves.
Gibbons can move like lightning."

"If the mother gibbon gets upset,
she might stop caring for her baby,"
said the young keeper.

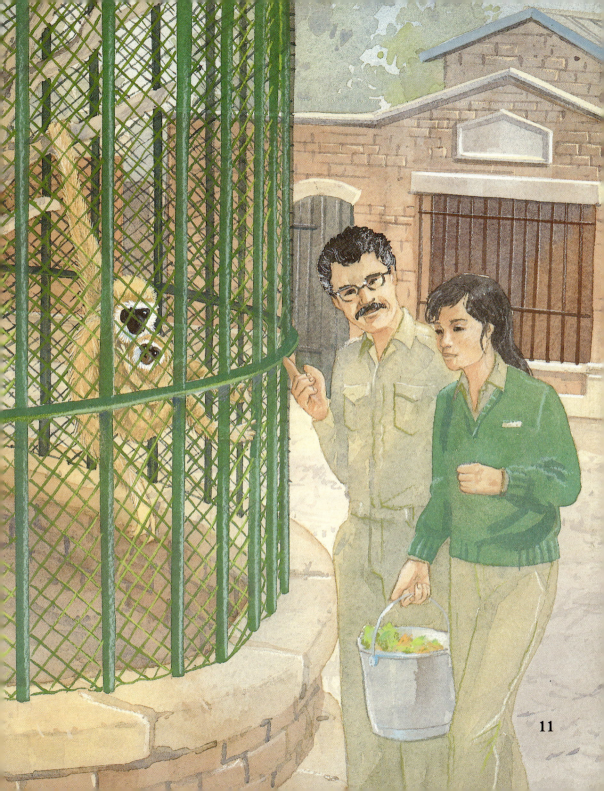

So, one morning, before the zoo was open,
a vet with a dart gun
put the gibbons to sleep for a while.

The keepers put nets around them
and took them down to the lake
in a truck.
When the gibbons woke up,
they were inside their new house.

"We want the gibbons to feel safe
before we let them out,"
said the head keeper.

All the next week,
the gibbons just **looked** at their island
through the big windows.

At last, the keepers opened the door.
They watched as the gibbons came out
and crossed the bridge to the island.

The gibbons were not at all scared!
They climbed the trees
and swung along the branches,
hand over hand.

And when the children came to the zoo,
they loved watching the gibbons
swinging from tree to tree.
"Gibbon Island
is their very own playground,"
they said.